DEADLY DISEASES
and Curious Cures

Anna Claybourne

Published 2010 by
A & C Black Publishers Ltd.
36 Soho Square, London, W1D 3QY
www.acblack.com

ISBN   HB 978-1-4081-2437-6
       PB 978-1-4081-2692-9

Series consultant: Gill Matthews

Produced for A & C Black by Calcium. www.calciumcreative.co.uk

Printed and bound in China by C&C Offset Printing Co.

Acknowledgements

The publishers would like to thank the following for their kind permission to reproduce their photographs:

Cover: Shutterstock **Pages:** Alamy Images: Medical-on-Line 25; Corbis: Historical Picture Archive 21; Getty Images: The Bridgeman Art Library 23t; Istockphoto: Grafissimo 28, Duncan Walker 13c; Library of Congress: 15; Photolibrary: 8b; Shutterstock: Rimantas Abromas 27tr, Potapov Alexander 19t, Khomulo Anna 12t, Subbotina Anna 4b, ANP 24t, Davi Sales Batista 10t, Betacam-SP 6t, Cartoonhead 29t, Andraž Cerar 6b, Charlotte Erpenbeck 19b, Lagui 5c, Ledo 24b, LilKar 14b, Lilun 29b, Polina Lobanova 18l, Milos Luzanin 22t, Reha Mark 10b, Originalpunkt 14t, Orionmystery 7b, Michael Pemberton 18r, Pennyimages 12bl, Psamtik 17b, Koum Quat 4t, Tom Robbrecht 27b, Elena Schweitzer 8t, 27tl, Shoeberl 22b, Roman Sigaev 23b, Stocksnapp 26, SVLumagraphica 9, Michael Taylor 20t, Tohan 16, 27c, Vinata 12br, Yasna 5t, Marlena Zagajewska 13t; Wikimedia Commons: 5b, 11, Gaius Cornelius 20b, Magnus Manske 17t, Forest & Kim Starr 7t.

Contents

Welcome Aboard!

Welcome to a life of danger, disaster, and deadly disease! As a ship's **surgeon** in the 1700s, you won't just hand out cough mixture and bandages. No, you'll fix broken bones, pull out teeth and burst boils. You will also chop off rotting legs, dig out bullets and sew up wounds. So you'd better have nerves of steel!

Your medicine chest

Every ship's surgeon needs a well-stocked medicine chest. Here are some of the things it should contain:

Medicines

- Aloe Vera
- Chamomile
- Cinnamon
- Clove oil
- Dragon's blood
- Hone
- Lavender
- Liquorice
- Mercury pills
- Mint
- Mustard
- Myrrh
- Opium
- Peppermint
- Peruvian Bark
- Rhubarb
- Rosemary
- Squill
- Turpentine
- Vinegar
- Wormwood

Mint

Tools and supplies

- bandages
- blood bowls
- **cauterizing** irons
- cloths
- **forceps**
- head saw
- knives and razors
- needles and thread
- pestle and mortar
- pliers
- **probes**
- scissors
- weighing scales

The surgeon's sickbay

Your ship has a special **sickbay**, where you can keep an eye on sailors who aren't feeling well. Each day you should:

- check on your patients
- prepare and hand out medicines
- do urgent operations
- keep the sickbay clean

Famous pirate Blackbeard once demanded a medicine chest in return for setting some hostages free!

Blackbeard knew his pirate crew were worth their weight in gold – and keeping them healthy was important.

Cabin Fever

As your ship sails the world, the sailors will pick up all kinds of nasty germs and bugs. These come from dirty water, bad food, and local people. Many of these germs cause a high temperature, or **fever**. Once the fever has passed, your patient may get better. But watch out for malaria. It can be a killer.

Fever treatments

Treat fever with one of these remedies.

Wormwood

This herb has been used since ancient times. Give the patient salts of wormwood, made from ashes collected after burning the plant.

Mercury

Pills containing **mercury** are a fever cure.

Vinegar

If you've run out of other medicines, try a spoonful of vinegar.

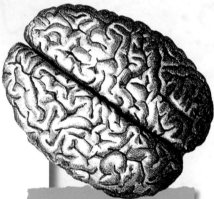

Fever affects the brain and can cause **hallucinations**.

Modern scientists know that mercury is actually a poison! But hundreds of years ago it was used as a medicine.

Mercury

Malaria treatment

The best malaria cure is Peruvian bark, from the cinchona tree. Here's how to use it:

1 Use dried, powdered Peruvian bark.

2 The patient will suffer high fevers with **chills** in between.

3 Give one grain of bark every hour during the chills.

The cinchona tree comes from South America.

Top Tips

Watch out for stripy mosquitoes like this. They're the ones that spread malaria when they suck your blood.

Terrible Toothache

There's no such thing as toothpaste, so you'll spend plenty of time looking at stinky, rotten teeth. Quite often, you'll have to pull them out too. Pliers at the ready!

Cloves are the dried flower buds of a type of tree.

Treatment for toothache

You will need:

- clove oil
- cloth

Surgeon skills

1 Soak the cloth in clove oil.
2 Fold it up tightly.
3 Press the cloth against the bad tooth, and shut the patient's mouth to hold it in place.

You'll need a firm grip to pull out some teeth!

Taking a tooth out

You will need:

- grippers or pliers
- cloth
- vinegar

Pliers

Surgeon skills

1 Use the pliers to grip the bad tooth firmly.

2 Lever and twist the tooth around to loosen it.

3 Be careful not to shatter the tooth or damage nearby healthy teeth!

4 Pull the tooth out.

5 Wash the mouth out with vinegar.

6 Use cloth to fill the gap and soak up the blood.

Bad teeth

Many 17th-century sailors have rotten teeth and bad breath. To make matters worse, diseases such as scurvy (see page 26) can make teeth go bad.

Falls and Fractures

Arrrrrgggggghh! THUD!!!
What was that?
It was probably
one of the sailors
falling off the **rigging**
and hitting the deck.
If he's survived, it is
likely he'll have horrible
injuries. You must be
ready to fix them.

Rigging

Setting a broken bone

You will need:

• a splint, such as a length of wood

• bandages

• painkilling medicine

Surgeon skills

1   Give the patient a painkiller, such as **opium** or rum.

2   Gently pull the broken arm or leg to straighten it. Ouch!

3   Lay the splint along the broken limb.

4   Bandage the splint to the limb tightly.

Fixing a smashed skull

You will need:

- cloths and seawater
- a knife or chisel
- a head saw or trepan
- bandages

Surgeon skills

1 Wash the head with seawater.

2 Pull out any smashed-in sections of skull and pick out splinters.

3 Use the head saw to cut off sticking-out pieces of bone.

4 If there is swelling, you must use the **trepan**. It will make a hole in the skull to release blood inside.

5 Bandage up the head.

The trepan drilled holes in a person's skull.

Man overboard!

Surprisingly, many sailors aren't good swimmers. If they go overboard, they begin to sink! To treat a drowning man, hold him upside down and shake him well to remove water from his lungs.

Tummy Bugs

On board ship you'll see lots of vomiting and diarrhoea. **Seasickness**, rotten food, and germs can give sailors tummy bugs. Luckily, you have lots of handy sickness medicines in your medicine chest.

A cure for vomiting

You can use flavoured water called "aquae" to treat sickness. You will need:

- ginger root, aniseed, cinnamon, or peppermint
- boiling water
- clean cloth

Surgeon skills

1 Stir the herb or root you are using into the hot water.

2 Leave the mixture to cool.

3 Strain the water through a cloth to remove the bits.

4 Give the patient a glass of the medicine every hour.

Peppermint and ginger (below) are both good for sickness.

Treating diarrhoea

Diseases such as **cholera** can cause diarrhoea as well as vomiting. To treat diarrhoea you will need:

• dried rhubarb

• wine

• cloths

Surgeon skills

1 Stir the rhubarb into the wine.

2 Give the patient a glass of the medicine, then send him to rest in bed.

3 Warm the cloths by the fire and lay them over the patient's stomach.

Lord Nelson

Seasick admiral

English admiral Lord Horatio Nelson spent his life at sea. Although he loved ships, he suffered from bad seasickness. He often had to stay in his bed for days on end.

You might think coughs and colds aren't that serious. But a nasty cold or flu bug is bad news at sea. It can put most of the crew out of action.

Medicine bottle

Syrup of squills cure

This cold **remedy** is made from a seashore plant called squill. It's good for chesty coughs, blocked noses, and sore throats. You will need:

- squill extract
- honey
- sugar

Surgeon skills

1 Stir the ingredients together to make a thick syrup.

2 Give the patient a large spoonful three times a day.

Honey has been used for centuries to soothe sore throats and kill germs.

Healing a headache

- Soak chamomile flowers in water to make a soothing drink.

- Place a warmed cup upside down on the head. As it cools, it will suck the skin. This is called "cupping". It is thought to cure all kinds of aches and pains.

- Try syrup of **ipecac**, which comes from a plant root. It will make your patient vomit, but his headache might go away!

Explorers spread dangerous cold and flu germs to the Taino people of the Caribbean in the 1490s.

Spreading germs

Explorers from Europe first sailed to the Americas in the late 1400s. They took cold and flu germs with them, and passed them to the local people. Many locals then died. They had never had these germs before and their bodies were not used to them.

Lancing a Boil

Boils happen when germs and dirt collect under the skin and swell up. Boils are common at sea, where sailors live crowded together in dirty conditions. Some boils get bigger and bigger until they POP! Others have to be **lanced**, or sliced open.

A ship makes a great home for boil germs!

Plaster for a boil

A **plaster** is an **ointment**-like mixture. You put one on a boil to make it come to the surface and burst. You will need:

• lard

• oil

• mustard

• a piece of cloth

Surgeon skills

1 Mix the ingredients together over a fire.

2 Smear the warm mixture on to the cloth.

3 Lay the cloth plaster-side down over the boil.

Lancing a boil

So the boil hasn't popped? It's time to lance it. You will need:

- seawater
- a small, sharp knife
- turpentine
- cloths
- bandage

Surgeon skills

1 Wash the area with seawater.

2 Slice the boil open with a knife and squeeze it.

3 Use the cloths to soak up the **pus** and blood. Yuck!

4 Wash the area with turpentine.

5 Bandage the wound until it heals over.

A boil oozes disgusting, yellow **pus**.

Turpentine is a good germ-killer, but warn your patient that it may sting and burn!

Turpentine is made of juice or sap from a pine tree.

Battle Wounds

A good ship's surgeon must always be ready for a pirate attack! With their razor-sharp swords and deadly guns, pirates can cause some nasty wounds. Even if your crew fights them off, you'll have lots of injuries to deal with.

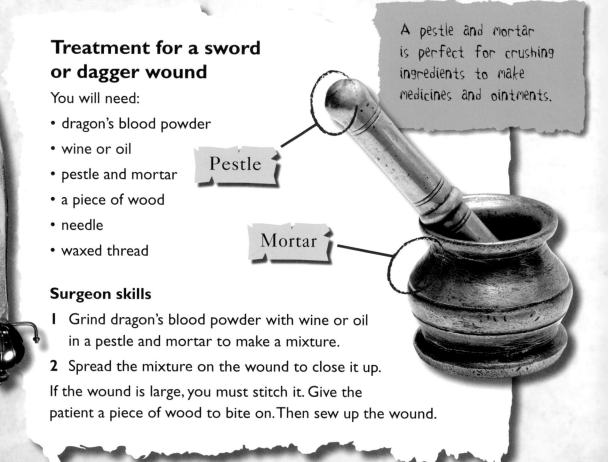

A pestle and mortar is perfect for crushing ingredients to make medicines and ointments.

Pestle

Mortar

Treatment for a sword or dagger wound

You will need:

- dragon's blood powder
- wine or oil
- pestle and mortar
- a piece of wood
- needle
- waxed thread

Surgeon skills

1 Grind dragon's blood powder with wine or oil in a pestle and mortar to make a mixture.

2 Spread the mixture on the wound to close it up.

If the wound is large, you must stitch it. Give the patient a piece of wood to bite on. Then sew up the wound.

Removing bullets

You will need:

- forceps
- a thin metal stick
- turpentine or vinegar
- bandage

Surgeon skills

1 Using the stick, poke around inside the wound until you find the bullet.

2 Use the forceps to grab the bullet and pull it out.

3 Clean the wound with turpentine or vinegar.

4 Bandage up the area to cover the bullet hole.

Dragon tree

"Dragon's blood" doesn't really come from dragons! It is made from the red juice of the dragon tree.

Rotten Wounds

Unfortunately, wounds don't always heal over well. If germs get inside, they can become **infected**. That means they swell up, hurt, and ooze yucky yellow pus. If **gangrene** sets in, whole body parts start to rot away!

Some bacteria are germs that infect wounds.

Plaster for an infected wound

You will need:

- lard
- olive oil
- dried lavender
- powdered myrrh
- clean cloth

Myrrh

Surgeon skills

1 Mix the ingredients together over a stove.

2 Smear the mixture on to a cloth.

3 Press the plaster against the infected wound, pressing it in well.

Bloodletting

Another treatment for infected wounds is bloodletting. This means to cause bleeding.

You will need:

- a sharp scalpel or knife
- a blood bowl

Make sure the patient is sitting down. Find a nice big **vein** in the arm and cut into it carefully with your **scalpel**. Catch the blood in the bowl.

Is it gangrene?

Look out for these signs of grisly gangrene:

- skin turns greenish-black
- flesh starts to cave in and rot
- wound smells really bad!

If it is gangrene, turn the page to find out how to CHOP IT OFF!

Bloodletting used to be a popular medical treatment. Sadly, it didn't work!

Off With His Leg!

Sometimes part of a sailor's body is very badly damaged by gangrene or an injury. Then it has to be **amputated**. That means chopping it right off. That's why you often see old pictures of pirates and sailors with wooden legs or hooks for hands.

How to amputate a leg

You will need:

- a tourniquet (strip of cloth)
- a scalpel
- an axe or saw
- a cauterizing iron
- bandages
- opium

Axe

If you had a limb amputated in the 1700s, you might still die from an infected stump, bleeding, or shock.

Saw

This old painting shows a ship **officer** about to have an amputation.

Surgeon skills

1 Give your patient plenty of opium or rum.

2 Lie him on a table with several men to hold him still.

3 Tie the **tourniquet** tightly round the leg above the wound, to reduce blood flow.

4 Cut the flesh around the bone with the scalpel.

5 Pull back the flesh so that the bone is sticking out.

6 Saw or chop through the bone.

7 Press a hot cauterizing iron against the stump. This stops the bleeding.

8 Wrap the stump tightly in bandages.

9 Give the patient more opium to reduce pain as he recovers.

Opium

Hot and Cold

Sailing ships can travel into the most swelteringly hot and shivering cold parts of the world. Getting too hot or cold can be harmful, and even deadly.

Weather remedies

Have these treatments ready whenever your ship encounters extreme weather.

1 Sunstroke

Sunstroke makes sailors dizzy, sick and faint with heat.
What to do: keep the patient in the shade, and use damp cloths to cool him down. Give him cold water to drink.

2 Sunburn

Sunburn makes the skin turn red, blister, and peel.
What to do: rub aloe vera juice all over the burned area.

Blazing sunshine could roast your crew!

Aloe vera

3 Exposure

Exposure means getting much too cold, from winter weather or falling into icy water.
What to do: put the sailor into a warm room. Remove his wet clothes and lay warm cloths all over him.

4 Frostbite

Frostbite happens when fingers and toes freeze and turn black.
What to do: amputate the parts.

Frostbite can make skin turn black.

Sailor hats!

Many old pictures of sailors and pirates show them wearing wide-brimmed hats, or handkerchiefs tied around their heads. These helped to protect them from sunburn and sunstroke.

Scary Scurvy

Many a sailing ship has lost half its men to a terrible illness – scurvy. It's caused by the poor diet that many sailors eat. If it's not treated, it's a killer. Luckily, there's a simple cure.

Spotting scurvy

Look out for these symptoms to see if scurvy is affecting the crew:

- aches and pains
- tiredness and weakness
- dark blotches and bruises
- pale skin
- loose teeth and bleeding gums

Top Tips

Give your crew pickled cabbage. It is very tasty and it is great for curing scurvy.

Captain James Cook gave his crew pickled cabbage to keep them healthy.

Cabbage

Scurvy treatment

You can cure scurvy by adding any of these foods to the patient's diet:

- Lemons, oranges, or limes
- Potatoes
- Cabbage

To prevent scurvy, the crew should eat fresh fruit and vegetables as much as possible, especially **citrus fruit** and **tamarind**.

Scurvy-busting food was prepared in the ship kitchen.

James Lind

Ship's captains and surgeons always knew that fresh food kept their men healthier. But it was only in the 1740s that British navy doctor James Lind proved that eating lemons and limes could get rid of scurvy.

All in the Mind

It's well known that sailors cooped up on board ship for months on end can go a little crazy. But don't worry – there are also medicines for this.

Are sailors' tales of sea monsters the result of strange visions?

Calenture

Sailors sometimes get **calenture** when their ships are stuck in one place with no wind. It makes them start seeing things. They may even leap overboard, because they think the sea is a green meadow!

Surgeon skills

1 Shut the patient safely in a cabin.

2 Give him a liquorice drink made by mixing liquorice and hot water.

3 If he doesn't recover, try bloodletting (see page 21).

Lizard

A cure for sleeplessness and terrors

To cure sleeplessness and fears, there is a very expensive medicine called theriac. It has a lot of ingredients, so most surgeons buy it ready-made from an **apothecary**. However, you could make a simple version using these ingredients:

- 1 dried snake
- 1 dried lizard
- Cinnamon
- Rhubarb
- Ginger
- Aniseed
- Pepper
- Cloves
- Myrrh
- Turpentine
- Opium
- Wine
- Honey

Grind and stir everything together, and give the patient a spoonful a day.

Top Tips

Opium is often used as a cure for worries and **depression**, as it sends you to sleep.

Opium is made from some types of poppy flowers.

Glossary

admiral commander of a fleet of ships

amputate to cut off a body part

apothecary someone who made and sold medicines

calenture an illness that makes people see things that aren't there

cauterize to seal up a wound with heat

chills feeling cold and shivery

cholera a serious disease spread by dirty drinking water

citrus fruit oranges, lemons, limes, grapefruits and similar fruit

depression an illness that makes people feel sad and hopeless

exposure (or hypothermia) the body getting too cold

fever a high body temperature

firearms guns and cannons

forceps tool for grabbing and holding

frostbite damage cause by body parts getting frozen

gangrene rotting away of living flesh

hallucination a terrible dream

hostage someone taken prisoner and released in exchange for something

infected invaded by disease germs

ipecac a plant that causes vomiting

lance to cut open

mercury a silvery metal that is a liquid at room temperature

officers those in charge on board ship

ointment thick, sticky medicine used on the skin

opium painkilling substance made from a type of poppy

plaster a creamy mixture of medicines for smearing on the skin

probe long needle-like tool

pus sticky yellow stuff that comes out of wounds

remedy a medical cure or treatment

rigging ropes used to hold up sails

scalpel small, sharp knife

seasickness feeling sick because of the movement of a boat

sickbay area of ship where unwell sailors are treated

sunstroke (or heatstroke) the body overheating

surgeon a doctor who can carry out operations

tamarind fruit of the tamarind tree, found in Asia

tourniquet a band tied around a body part to slow down bleeding

trepan a drill-like tool for making holes in the skull

vein a type of blood vessel or tube inside the body

further Information

Books

Sail!: Can You Command a Sea Voyage? by Julia Bruce. Enslow Publishers (2009).

A Year on a Pirate Ship by Elizabeth Havercroft. Millbrook Press (2009).

Powder Monkey: The Adventures of Sam Witchall by Paul Dowswell. Bloomsbury (2008).

Renaissance Medicine by Ian Dawson. Wayland (2005)

Doctors Did What?!: The Weird History of Medicine by Richard Platt. Two-Can Publishers (2006).

Index